Dedicated To:
Fr. Edward Ahn

Written By: Abigail Gartland

Hello, my name is St. Anthony!

I was born in Portugal in the year 1195.

When I was 15, I moved into an Abbey where I learned about the faith.

I studied hard there and became a priest. I joined the Franciscan Friars.

I loved being a Franciscan so much that I started my own order of priests.

One day, I was spreading the word of God and became very sick.

I went back home to rest and get better. I spent my time studying and praying.

One day, as I was praying, I realized that my special book of prayers was missing.

I prayed and prayed, asking God to help me, and I found it!

I thanked Jesus that He helped me find m[y] important book.

I am always pictured holding a child. This shows my love for the infant, Jesus.

Do you want to be more like me?

You can celebrate my feast day with me on June 13th.

I am the patron saint of lost things

If you ever lose something you can pray for St. Anthony's help:

"Tony Tony, look around. Something is lost and must be found."

I pray for you every day of your life.

St. Anthony, pray for us!

Copyright:

Clipart: © PentoolPixie © LimeandKiwiDesigns
Licensed purchased: 1/10/2024

About the Author

Abigail Gartland

I love the saints and I love my faith. The idea for sharing the stories of the saints with little ones came when my dear friends were expecting their first baby. I wanted to create something as unique and special as our friendship. Each book is dedicated to very special people and groups who have enriched my faith in different ways. I am blessed to write these stories and appreciate the unending support of my family and friends. When I am not writing, I am a middle school teacher. I hope you enjoy these stories. I pray for each and every person who opens one of my books to learn more about the saints.

Abbie

www.ingramcontent.com/pod-product-compliance
Lightning Source LLC
LaVergne TN
LVHW052047070526
838201LV00087B/4909